Anytime I've been sad or happy
or really mad about something,

POKÉMON HAVE
ALWAYS BEEN THERE

by my side, through it all.

" "

ASH

The Essential

POKÉMON™

Book of Joy

DEL REY

2016 Del Rey Trade Paperback Edition

Published in the United States by Del Rey, an imprint of Random House,
a division of Penguin Random House LLC, New York.

DEL REY and the HOUSE colophon are registered trademarks
of Penguin Random House LLC.

Published in the United Kingdom by Century, an imprint of Penguin Random House UK.

ISBN 978-0-399-18148-1

Printed in the United States of America on acid-free paper

randomhousebooks.com

2 4 6 8 9 7 5 3 1

Designed by Scott Biel and Amber Bennett-Ford

Yes, Pokémon evolve, and their Trainers grow older – but while everything changes, one thing remains true always. FRIENDS CAN BE FRIENDS FOREVER, and even if they seem a little different, sometimes you have to *look with your heart* and not your eyes.

" "

NARRATOR

CONTENTS

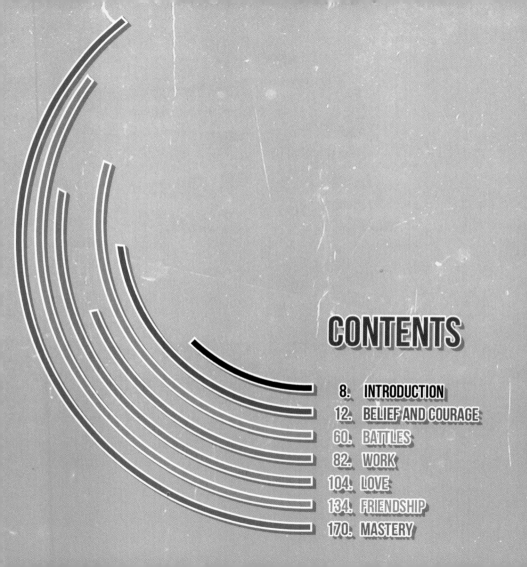

CONTENTS

DEAR READER,

Like our heroes Ash and Pikachu, we are all on a road to personal mastery. Whether we want to become the greatest Trainer in the world, to develop into a more powerful being, or just to become the best versions of ourselves, we are all at different points along life's winding path.

But like the seasoned Pokémon Trainer who has thrown too many Poké Balls to count, our journey in life is never easy. For every battle won, a battle elsewhere is lost. For every Jigglypuff evolved, an Igglybuff is forever changed. For every inspirational Brock we meet, a Team Rocket member is lurking in the bushes, ready to pounce.

During the tough times in life, we must be calm and good-spirited. Like Ash, we must believe in ourselves and play to our strengths. Our journey may be long, and we must exercise patience. If we move too quickly, we will go backward, not forward. Only if we rely on the kindness of others, and if we cherish our friends, will we make our lives our most wonderful adventures.

This book's wisdom has been amassed over the course of many adventures across the Pokémon world. Within its chapters you will discover simple but powerful philosophies that can change every aspect of your life. From tender expressions of love and friendship to inspiring aphorisms to follow your dreams; from hard-fought lessons about failure to sage advice on victory and happiness. Whether through the machinations of Team Rocket, the moral fortitude of our heroes, or anything in between, one thing is clear: any situation faced is an opportunity to learn!

I urge you to read this book, to cherish its wisdom, and to act out its philosophy as much as you can in your daily life. For remember: a heart can be so true that our courage will pull us through!

ANONYMOUS

Chapter 1

BELIEF & COURAGE

I WANNA BE THE VERY BEST

like no one ever was.

" "

POKÉMON THEME

FOCUS ON
THE HERE AND NOW.

It's the first day of
the rest of your life.

" "

MEOWTH

When you got **lemons**, you make **lemonade**;
and when you got **rice**, you make **rice balls**.

" "

BROCK

We're all on the road to make our

dreams come true.

FULL SPEED AHEAD!

" "

A S H

The first thing you need to do is

CALM YOUR MIND.

If you observe closely with a calm mind, you'll be able to

discern the *important things.*

" "

RAMOS

I'VE GOTTA KEEP GOING!

Keep...going...going...gone...

I've gotta work out more often.

" "

MEOWTH

You're always putting me down, but I'll show you!
I'm gonna prove to you

I CAN DO IT! I'M GONNA BE A POKÉMON MASTER! STAND BACK AND WATCH ME WORK!

" "

ASH

THE FUTURE LOOKS BRIGHT

for our heroes now, but up ahead, Viridian Forest is deeper and darker than they know.... And a dangerous

NEW CHALLENGE IS WAITING!

" "

NARRATOR

JUST KEEP ON DOING YOUR BEST.

" "

MISTY

Adventure Rule Number Four:

YOU NEVER GIVE UP UNTIL THE VERY END!

Cause there's always gotta be a way out. You get it?!

" "

ASH

CRYIN'

DON'T HELP.

I already tried that.

" "

MEOWTH

I want my Pikachu to be the

BEST POKÉMON IT CAN

POSSIBLY BE.

" "

ASH

TAKE ON EVERY CHALLENGE

...and rise above them all!

" "

GRACE

What adventures will our friends find along the way?
Those answers aren't yet written in stone!

" "

NARRATOR

REMEMBER, I'M
THE TOP CAT. MEOWTH!

" "

MEOWTH

No, *that's not possible.*

UNLESS, **OF COURSE, IT IS.**

" "

CEDRIC JUNIPER

Whining *only makes you* **hungrier.**

" "

MEOWTH

A HEART SO TRUE OUR COURAGE WILL PULL US THROUGH.

" "

POKÉMON THEME

BIG SMILES AND EVEN BIGGER HOPES

for a future that's cleaner and greener than before.

" "

NARRATOR

I will travel across the land
Searching far and wide
Each Pokémon to understand
The power that's inside.

" "

POKÉMON THEME

JUST BE CONFIDENT.

*You can do anything you
set your mind to.*

" "

DELIA KETCHUM

Every **challenge** along the way
With **courage** I will face.
I will **battle** every day
To **claim** my rightful place.

" "

POKÉMON THEME

PIKA, PIKA!

" "

PIKACHU

Chapter 2

BATTLES

Prepare for *trouble*, and make it double

To *protect* the world from devastation,

To *unite* all peoples within our nation,

To *denounce* the evils of truth and love,

To *extend* our reach to the stars above

JESSIE! JAMES!

Team Rocket blasts off at the speed of light.

Surrender now or prepare to fight.

MEOWTH, that's right!

" "

TEAM ROCKET

If you get all caught up with the things

that are right in front of you,

YOU MAY LOSE SIGHT OF WHAT'S

IMPORTANT.

" "

RAMOS

Feeling frustrated? Then use all that frustration and

GET OUT THERE!

Do it!

" "

A S H

Hey, chill out kid, cool your flame!
Now, who would want to have fisticuffs

ON A NICE MOONLIT NIGHT
LIKE THIS?

" "

MEOWTH

We studied for the big test.

So sure we would beat all the rest.

Here's the part I like the best: we frolicked that night,

for our future seemed bright. But things weren't right...

We got the lowest scores in the history of the school!

" "

JESSIE AND JAMES, TEAM ROCKET

USE MORE THAN ONE POKÉMON IF YOU'RE AFRAID TO LOSE.

" "

GIOVANNI

THIS POKÉMON'S GOT GUTS!

My guts are busting...

" "

MEOWTH

LOSING IS VERY IMPORTANT, ISN'T IT?

Losing is so important, it's what we
based our whole career on!

" "

JAMES AND MEOWTH, TEAM ROCKET

When fortune smiles on you,

YOU JUST SMILE ON BACK.

" "

JESSIE, TEAM ROCKET

We may be mean and nasty, but we'd

NEVER TURN OUR BACKS

ON A TEAMMATE IN TROUBLE.

" "

JESSIE, TEAM ROCKET

Chapter 3

WORK

The progress of science stops the moment you give up.

IF YOU DON'T GIVE UP,

ANYTHING IS POSSIBLE!

" "

CLEMONT

MINIMAL EFFORT **WITH** MAXIMUM PROFIT!

That's the Team Rocket way!

" "

TEAM ROCKET

THINGS WON'T JUST WORK OUT IF YOU TRY HARD ENOUGH.

The Pokémon Trainer's judgment is more important than anything else.

" "

MISTY

If we all

DANCE TOGETHER,

it'll be more fun!

" "

SERENA

A STRATEGY –

so they've been planning a new way to lose.

" "

LT. SURGE

EVERYTHING TAKES TIME, MAGIKARP

It took me three years
to grow this mustache.

" "

QUINCY

There are some things
you just can't learn at school,
and that's a good lesson.

" "

GISELLE

THERE'S NO HARM IF WE SLOW IT DOWN

just a little bit!

" "

ASH

We may not make a lot of money, but we sure have

GOT OUR FREEDOM.

" "

JESSIE

You should mind your

P'S AND Q'S AND PIKACHUS.

" "

MEOWTH

Chapter 4

LOVE

*It seems the world **I'm looking for** and the world you're looking for **are not the same...***

BUT WE CAN STILL GET ALONG!

" "

N

There's nothing wrong with wanting to hold onto precious things from the past. But becoming overly attached can keep yo

STUCK IN THE PAST.

" "

WOODWARD

A REAL GENTLEMAN ALWAYS CARRIES THE BAG.

" "

JESSIE, TEAM ROCKET

She looks just like all the other Joys...

YEAH, IT'S A JOY-FUL WORLD.

" "

MISTY AND ASH

YOU THINK PEOPLE CHANGE
WHEN THEY GET KISSED?

I guess we'll have to find out ourselves.

" "

ASH AND MISTY

A LITTLE POKÉMON
LOVE POWER
works miracles!

" "

CASSIDY

*You **can't judge a Pokémon** by its smell.*

" "

NARRATOR

Men!

They always try to project their insecurity onto girls.

" "

MAY

IT TAKES COURAGE TO APOLOGIZE AFTER A FIGHT.

But we'll all be there cheering you on!

" "

CILAN

IT'S A LOT EASIER TO

LIKE SOMEONE WHO LIKES YOU

than to like someone who doesn't.

" "

MISTY

We believe in love power,

THAT'S

because we love power.

" "

CASSIDY AND BUTCH

LOOKS LIKE FRIENDSHIP'S STRONGER THAN JEALOUSY.

" "

BROCK

IT'S OK IF WE'RE NOT PERFECT.

" "

SERENA

PIKACHU, I CHOOSE YOU!

" "

ASH

Chapter 5

FRIENDSHIP

Come with me, the **time** is right

There's no better **team**

Arm in arm we'll win the **fight**

It's always been our **dream**.

" "

POKÉMON THEME

If you two had spent less time arguing and paid more attention to where we're going, we'd already be

IN VERMILLION CITY

by now.

" "

BROCK

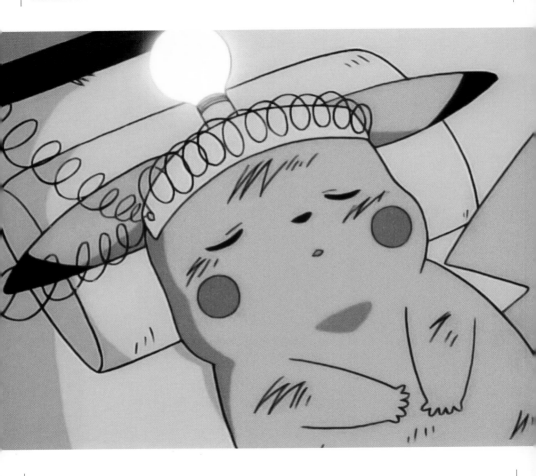

All I know is that my buddy Pikachu and all Pokémon are

FRIENDS THAT I CARE A LOT ABOUT!

" "

ASH

We've been together since you were
Charmander and then when you evolved
into Charmeleon — and all I want to do is

BE GOOD ENOUGH FOR YOU
SO WE CAN BATTLE
SIDE BY SIDE AS A TEAM.

" "

ASH

CHARACTER IS ANOTHER WORD FOR TROUBLEMAKER...

" "

MAY

We are only going to have smiles from here on in.
This is the place where

THE FUN NEVER ENDS.

" "

WATTSON

If we learn as much as we can about Pokémon, then that will help us become

BETTER FRIENDS

with them!

" "

ASH

There's *nothing* we could *ever* do that's

A WASTE OF TIME!

" "

ASH

I think we were meet to meet and

BECOME FRIENDS.

" "

ASH

Our *new challenge* *is*

JUST BEGINNING,

right, Pikachu?!

" "

ASH

WITH ENEMIES LIKE THAT, WHO NEEDS FRIENDS?

" "

JAMES, TEAM ROCKET

I THINK PIKACHU'S A GREAT POKÉMON

just the way it is.

" "

ASH

It's better to

MAKE UP QUICKLY AFTER A FIGHT

rather than drag it out.

" "

CILAN

The longer you wait, the harder it'll be for

EITHER OF YOU

to apologize!

" "

CILAN

All that 'making them serve us' stuff...

I DON'T KNOW ABOUT ANY OF THAT!

" "

ASH

RECOGNIZE WHAT'S IN EACH OTHER'S HEARTS.

That's what counts.

" "

OFFICER JENNY

You've got

BUDDIES WHO'D

give you the shirts off their backs if you needed

THEM.

" "

MEOWTH

Chapter 6

MASTERY

I WILL JOURNEY TO GAIN THE WISDOM OF POKÉMON TRAINING.

" "

ASH

DON'T TRY TO CHASE AFTER IT.

Relax, and let it come to you.

" "

ASH

DON'T THINK OF IT AS FAILING. THINK OF IT AS NOT SUCCEEDING!

" "

MEOWTH

Being your own Trainer

MUST BE

tough.

" "

A S H

Being nervous is only natural. I was always that way before a race. And that's when you need to tell yourself:

IT'S TIME TO GO FOR BROKE!

" "

GRACE

FAILURE LEADS TO SUCCESS!

That's how truly great inventions get perfected.

" "

LILIA

If I really think about it, I'd rather do stuff! 'Cause

EVEN IF I GOOF UP, I LEARN SOMETHING.

" "

A S H

Thinking too much won't help. **For now, I've got to**

KEEP MOVING FORWARD!

" "

S E R E N A

We haven't lost anything yet!

THERE'S NO REASON TO GIVE UP!

" "

ASH

PIKACHU!

" "

PIKACHU

Bibliography

All quotes in this book are sourced from the Pokémon animated series, licensed by
The Pokémon Company International, Inc.

p.1. Ash and N: A Clash of Ideals!; p.5. Showdown at Linoone; p.15. Pokémon Theme; p.16. Tears for Fears!; p.19. Pokémon Paparazzi; p.20. Dreaming a Performer's Dream!; p.23. The Green, Green Grass Types of Home; p.24. So You're Having a Bad Day!; p.27. Mystery at the Lighthouse!; p.28. Ash Captures a Pokémon!; p.31. Gotta Catch You Later!; p.32. Team Plasma and the Awakening Ceremony; p.35. A Shroomish Skirmish; p.36. The Case of the K-9 Caper; p.39. A Race for Home!; p.40. Haunter vs. Kadabra; p.43. Pokémon Showdown; p.44. Ash and N: A Clash of Ideals!; p.47. Pokémon Shipwreck; p.48. Pokémon Theme; p.51. Sparks Fly for Magnemite!; p. 52. Pokémon Theme; p.55. Pokémon Showdown; p. 56. Pokémon Theme; p.59. Showdown in Pewter City; p.63. Pokémon Emergency; p.64. The Green, Green Grass Types of Home; p.67. A Rush of Ninja Wisdom!; p.68. Tears for Fears!; p.71. The School of Hard Knocks; p.72. The Battle of the Badge; p.75. So You're Having a Bad Day!; p.76. The Mandarin Island Miss-Match; p.79. So You're Having a Bad Day!; p.80. Go West, Young Meowth!; p.85. A Watershed Moment!; p.86. Mantine Overboard!; p.89. Ash Captures a Pokémon!; p.90. A Frolicking Find in the Flowers!; p.93. Electric Shock Showdown; p.94. The Wacky Watcher; p.97. The School of Hard Knocks; p.98 A Ruin with a View; p.101. Holy Matrimony!; p.102. The Wacky Watcher; p.107. The Name's N!; p.108. Mending a Broken Spirit!; p.111. The Path to the Pokémon League; p.112. Charmander, the Stray Pokémon; p.115. Wherefore Art Thou, Pokémon; p.116. The Training Center Secret; p.119. Pokémon Scent-Sation; p.120. The Bicker the Better; p.123. The Path that Leads to Goodbye!; p.124. The Heartbreak of Brock; p.127. The Training Center Secret; p.129. Chikorita's Big Upset; p.130. Master Class Choices; p.132. The Water Flowers of Cerulean City; p.137. Pokémon Theme; p.138. The School of Hard Knocks; p.141. Ash and N: A Clash of Ideals!; p.142. Charizard Chills!; p.145. A Corphish Out of Water; p.146. Watt's with Wattson; p.149. Ash and N: A Clash of Ideals!; p.150. Performing a Pathway to the Future!; p.153. Gotta Catch Ya Later!; p.154. Kalos, Where Dreams and Adventures Begin!; p.157. The Song of Jigglypuff!; p.158. The Case of the K-9 Caper; p.161. The Path that Leads to Goodbye!; p.162. The Path that Leads to Goodbye!; p.165. Ash and N: A Clash of Ideals!; p.166. The Case of the K-9 Caper; p.169. Clamperl of Wisdom; p.173. Pokémon, I Choose You!; p.174. Wired for Battle; p.177. The Ultimate Test!; p.178. Who Gets to Keep Togepi?; p.181. Master Class Is in Session!; p.182. A Keeper for Keeps?; p.185. Performing a Pathway to the Future!; p.186. Master Class Choices!; p.188. The Cave of Mirrors!; p.190. Pokémon, I Choose You!